Screws

BY LYN SIROTA • ILLUSTRATED BY REGINALD BUTLER

Published by The Child's World®
1980 Lookout Drive • Mankato, MN 56003-1705
800-599-READ • www.childsworld.com

Acknowledgments
The Child's World®: Mary Berendes, Publishing Director
The Design Lab: Cover and interior design
Amnet: Cover and interior production
Red Line Editorial: Editorial direction

Photo credits
Dreamstime, cover, 1; Shutterstock Images, 9; iStockphoto, 11; Hintau Aliaksei/Shutterstock Images, 13; Jiri Hera/Shutterstock Images, 15; Winston Link/Shutterstock Images, 17; Bombaert Patrick/Shutterstock Images, 18; Christina Richards/Shutterstock Images, 21

Design elements: In.light/Dreamstime

Copyright © 2013 by The Child's World®
All rights reserved. No part of this book may be reproduced or utilized in any form or by any means without written permission from the publisher.

ISBN 9781614732761
LCCN 2012933655

Printed in the United States of America
Mankato, MN
July 2012
PA02120

ABOUT THE AUTHOR
Lyn Sirota is the author of 17 children's books and writes for various children's magazines. She is a regular contributor to *Science Weekly* and lives with her husband, children, and furry rescues.

ABOUT THE ILLUSTRATOR
Reginald Butler is a professional artist whose work includes poetry, painting, design, animation, commercial graphics, and music. One day he hopes to wake up and read his comic in the paper while watching his cartoon on television.

Table of Contents

Tools and Machines 4
A Kind of Ramp 6
Parts of a Screw 8
Spinning Circles 10
Thread Power 12
Pitch 14
Screws and Bolts 16
In Complex Machines 20
Screws Everywhere 22
    Glossary 24
    Books and Web Sites 24
    Index 24

Tools and Machines

What would your life be like without tools and machines? You use tools and machines every day. Tools and machines help you **work**. Computers are machines that help you store information. Cars are machines that help you move from place to place. Washing machines help you clean your clothes. These machines have many moving parts. Machines with many moving parts are **complex**. Complex machines are made up of many simple machines. There are six types of simple machines. They are screws, inclined planes, wedges, levers, wheels, and pulleys. It's time to learn about screws. Let's get to work!

You use simple machines even when you play outside.

A Kind of Ramp

An inclined plane is usually just a straight, slanted surface connecting two different levels. Think of a slide on the playground. A screw is different, though. A screw's ramp is wrapped around a tube. Screws help lock things together. They can hold heavy things up, too.

Inclined planes and screws are related.

Parts of a Screw

Screws have three parts. The head is on top. The **cylinder** is the long middle. The point is the end. The thread is the inclined plane part. The thread wraps around the cylinder.

EARLY SCREWS
The first screws made in a factory were not pointed at the end. A person had to drill a hole before the screw would go into a surface.

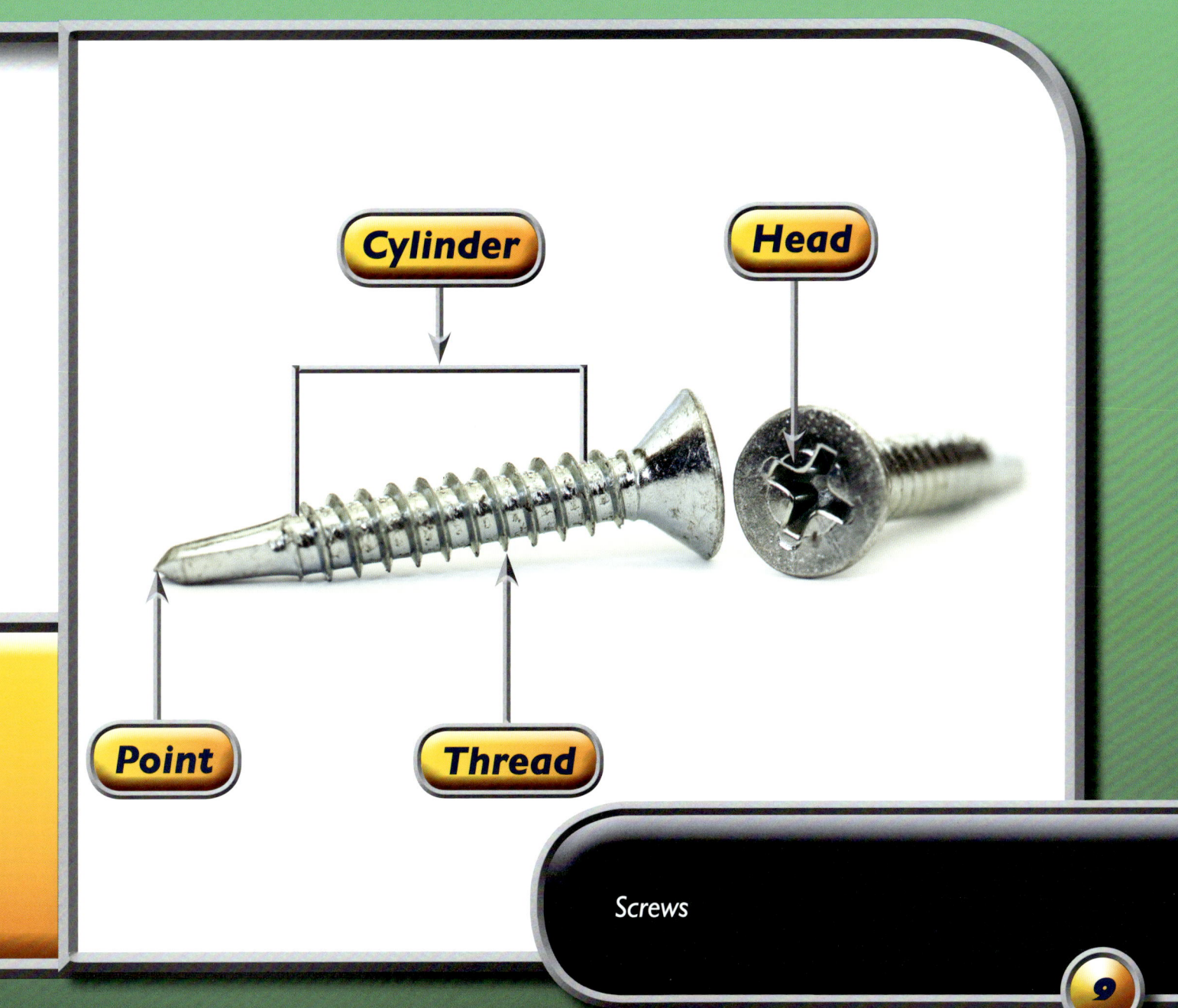

Screws

Spinning Circles

Turning a screw in a circle moves it farther into the object it is going into. The slanted thread of the screw is what helps it go deeper. The deeper the screw goes, the more **secure** the object is.

A screwdriver is used to turn a screw.

Thread Power

A screw's thread is what gives the screw power. The thread helps the screw hold things better than a nail. A nail has a straight cylinder without a thread. A nail goes deep. But it will not be as secure as a screw because its cylinder is smooth.

Imagine you have a heavy picture to hang on the wall. Do you think a nail or a screw will hold it better? A screw, of course!

The thread makes a screw more secure than a nail.

Pitch

Pitch is important for screws. The pitch of a screw is the amount of space between the thread. When the pitch is small, the thread is closer together. This makes a tighter hold.

But close threads mean more turning to get the screw into the surface. More work needs to be done in order to make the screw more secure.

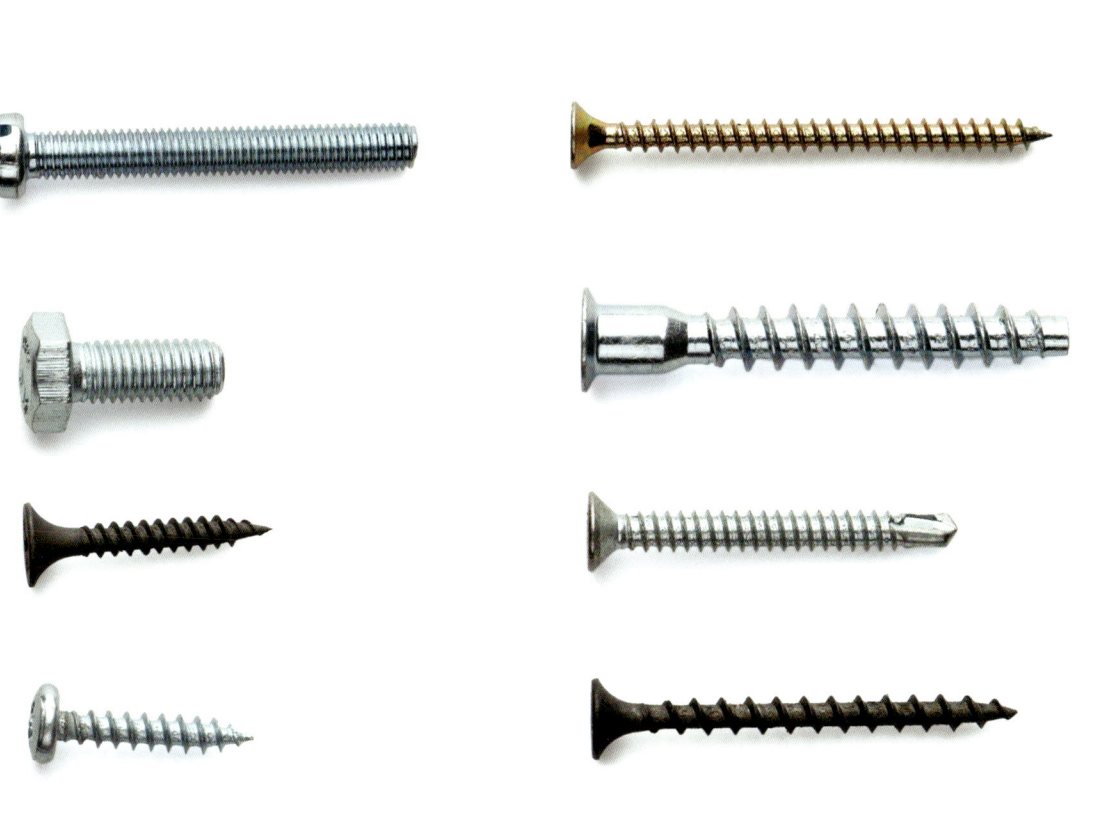

Screws come in many different pitches.

Screws and Bolts

Screws are related to bolts. Bolts have threads, too. Screws and bolts help keep objects locked together. However, screws can be used by themselves. Bolts are used with other pieces called nuts to hold things together.

SCREW HEADS

Screw heads do not all look the same. One may have an X on it. Another may just have a line. Each type of head needs a different type of screwdriver.

Nuts screw onto bolts.

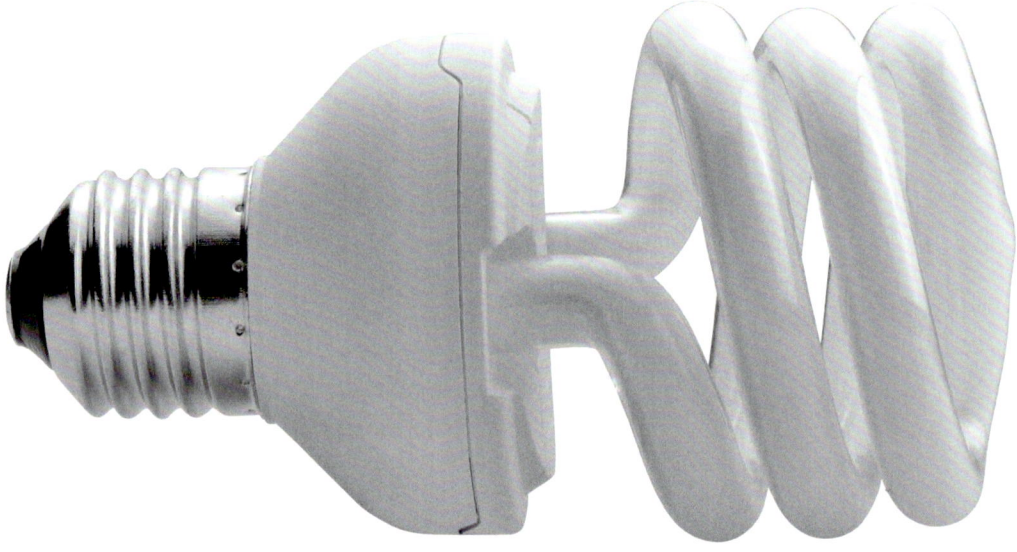

A screw is at the bottom of a light bulb.

Do you have jars in your cabinets or refrigerator? Look on the top edge of a jar. Do you see the thread? When you turn the lid on your jam jar, the thread helps the lid get nice and tight.

Have you ever changed a light bulb? If so, you would have seen a screw on it. The screw tightens the light bulb into place so you can have a bright room for reading.

In Complex Machines

Screws are used in many complex machines to keep parts together. You can find screws in cars, farming equipment, and computers. Wherever two objects need to be locked together on a machine, you will probably find a screw.

A man turns a screw in a computer.

21

Screws Everywhere

Now you know about screws. These simple machines are everywhere! They are behind your family portrait on the wall. They are inside lamps. Where else in your home can you find screws?

Hanging pictures use the strength of screws to stay up on the wall.

GLOSSARY

complex (kuhm-PLEKS): If something is complex, it has a lot of parts. A car is a complex machine.

cylinder (SIL-uhn-dur): A cylinder is a long, straight, solid object formed in the shape of a circle. The cylinder of the screw is the long body inside the thread.

secure (si-KYOOR): If something is secure, it is steady and strong. A screw is secure when it is completely in a piece of wood or metal.

work (WURK): Work is applying a force, such as pulling or pushing, to move an object. You do work when you turn a screwdriver.

BOOKS

Challen, Paul. *Get to Know Screws*. New York: Crabtree Publishing Company, 2009.

Gosman, Gillian. *Screws in Action*. New York: PowerKids Press, 2011.

Thompson, Gare. *Lever, Screw, and Inclined Plane: The Power of Simple Machines*. Washington, DC: National Geographic, 2006.

WEB SITES

Visit our Web site for links about screws:
childsworld.com/links

Note to Parents, Teachers, and Librarians: We routinely verify our Web links to make sure they are safe and active sites. So encourage your readers to check them out!

INDEX

bolts, 16
complex machines, 4, 20
inclined planes, 4, 6, 8
parts of screws, 8
pitch, 14
power, 12
simple machines, 4, 22
thread, 8, 10, 12, 14, 16, 19
work, 4, 14